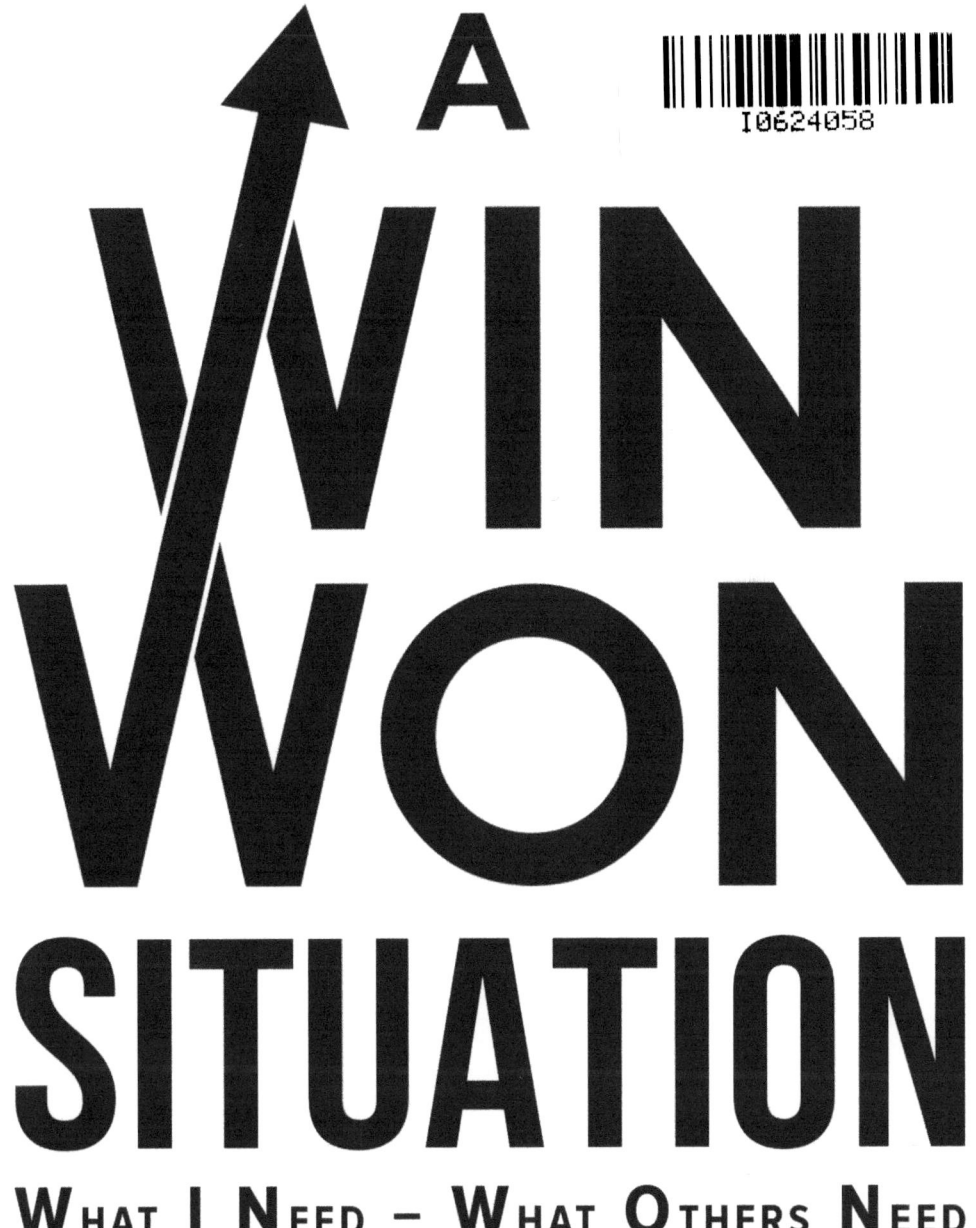

A
WIN
WON
SITUATION

WHAT I NEED – WHAT OTHERS NEED

A WIN WON SITUATION

WHAT I NEED – WHAT OTHERS NEED

REGGIE GRAY

Published by:
ELITE ONLINE PUBLISHING
63 East 11400 South
Suite #230
Sandy, UT 84070
EliteOnlinePublishing.com

ISBN - 978-1-961801-39-4 (Paperback)
ISBN - 978-1-961801-28-8 (Hardback)
ISBN - 978-1-961801-26-4 (eBook)
ISBN - 978-1-961801-30-1 (Audiobook)

BUS074040
BUS074030
SEL027000

QUANTITY PURCHASES: Schools, companies, professional groups, clubs,
and other organizations may qualify for special terms when ordering quantities of
this title. For information, email info@eliteonlinepublishing.com.

DEDICATION

Thank you to everyone who's come across my path and, in some way, contributed to this book and other books that may follow. You are part of these stories and contributed to molding my character, especially to the family and friends close to me and what you've either had to endure or enjoy by being a part of my life.

Most of all, to my sons, Remington, Royce, and Keller, thank you for motivating me every day to be better and do better so that you will be proud of me. And you already know, but I remind you, as I have for years, *you are the oxygen in my lungs.*

TABLE OF CONTENTS

Foreword vii

Introduction xiii

1 – Won 1

2 - Timing is Everything 5

3 – Time Out 13

4 – Us vs Them .21

5 – Viewpoint 37

6 – Communication is Key 45

7 – Quicksand 55

8 – It's Personal 59

9 - You Get What You Pay For 69

10 – Wait for It.... 75

11 - Decisions 83

12 - Stick to the Plan 97

About the Author 119

FOREWORD

I met Reggie more than 15 years ago while serving as the Assistant Special Agent in Charge (executive manager) for the Federal Bureau of Investigation (FBI) in Houston, Texas and had oversight of the Citizen's Academy Program. At the time, Reggie was president of the FBI Houston's Citizens Academy Alumni Association. He played a critical role building the nascent group on his gravitas and interpersonal skills, managing disparate personalities and personal agendas. At times it was like herding cats as they say. We first worked together when Reggie oversaw the Alumni Association's role in planning the official ribbon cutting ceremony opening FBI Houston's new building. While Reggie demonstrated great organizational skills, what immediately impressed me most were his charm and indefatigable energy.

Reggie always knew the right people and was in the right place at the right time.

During the years before I retired, my friendship with Reggie grew because I found him to be a man of impeccable character who was well placed in the community and genuinely wanted to be of service to the FBI and do the right thing. On numerous occasions I reached out to Reggie for help in meeting community leaders and bridging the gap between law enforcement and the public. Reggie regularly invited me to community and chamber events to expand and enhance my community involvement. During these functions, I observed Reggie's effusive positivity as critical to his personal success and noticed people found his charisma alluring. It was easily apparent he was well liked and highly respected. People genuinely enjoyed being in Reggie's company. His convivial nature and business knowledge were equally enchanting.

Following retirement, Reggie asked me to join the Intercontinental Chamber of Commerce's Board as an ex-officio member, and I later served executive chair. During my time with the chamber, I observed Reggie's true altruism and selflessness. He continually put the interests of the chamber and its members before his own. No opportunity to provide assistance was ever too large or small. Reggie's compassion for others was evidenced every day, manifested by his sincere desire to help others. For example, without hesitation he sprang into action and traveled to the Dominican Republic to assist a Houstonian wrongfully arrested for drug trafficking. Reggie leveraged his law enforcement and legal community connections to help bring the man back home. During Covid, Reggie used his contacts in China to secure personal protective equipment (PPE) like masks and gloves for governments who had difficulty obtaining the equipment because of the excessive demand at the time.

Reggie refocused the chamber from a business model of mass membership and refined it to a boutique chamber with fewer members that enabled him to provide a greater level of service and forge closer relationships between members. He is a great example of a transformational and servant leader. The success of the chamber was built on Reggie's shoulders. Reggie saw the need to expand the chamber internationally to meet the needs of its members more effectively. Reggie traveled the world building relationships with international business leaders and grew business to business relationships for chamber members. His easy-going style and communication abilities transcended language differences and dissolved international boundaries. Like Atlas carried the world on his shoulders, Reggie carried the chamber and its members across the globe. At times, Reggie's adventures resemble a James Bond novel with the good guy always coming out on top and fighting for what is right.

Reggie is a relationship builder, a connector who brings people together to build their enterprises and expand profitability. Once again, Reggie knows everyone, from community leaders to politicians to captains of industry. I often think everyone wishes they had Reggie's Rolodex. Everywhere he travels, building effective relationships and bringing people together are his goals. I observed Reggie treating everyone with respect, whether the custodian, corporate executive or powerful politician. Always the humble man no matter how large his success.

Reggie Gray represents all that is good in business: altruism, selflessness, synergistic relationships, building value for others and creating success.

There is so much we all can learn from Reggie and benefit from his experiences, travels and relationship building. The future is bright with Reggie traveling the globe advancing the chamber's mission for its members. You will enjoy his anecdotes and stories of self-shaping, life-shaping and legacy building.

– Michael E. Anderson, MBA, CFE
Retired FBI

INTRODUCTION

G etting Started…

I've contemplated writing about many issues, projects, or adventures for quite some time. Some of the delay was getting the time to focus. Still, most of it was the hesitation of releasing my personal stories and endeavors. Although it may not seem so to people who follow me on social media, etc., I stay as private as possible. So, to open my stories and my life and share them, it has been a decision to wait till my "Last 1/3," as I call it.

Life is divided into thirds. If one estimates an average life expectancy of 75, the first 25 years are learning and shaping yourself. The second 25 years are about shaping and experiencing your life, and the last 25 years are about leaving a legacy and enjoying the results of the first 50 years. I will get into more detail about time in a later chapter.

For the reader, understand that these stories and more will be in my second book, have been over years and at different stages in my life. I grew up in a religious family with strong faith, but that does not mean I've been a saint. One of the first things I do, like I'm doing now, is give my disclaimer. I'm telling you things as an example, but more of the statement, yes, I'm a rouge, I'm guilty, I did it, and I tried it. So, if you're reading to find faults, I have plenty. Let's get that understood and out of the way immediately.

My experiences allowed me to provide advice and learn about what I advise. I think the best summary could be that through all of it, my faith stayed, and even in my biggest disappointments and failures, I always could feel the forgiveness and love of who I refer to as God.

These chapters on different topics will impact your views and motivate or assist you in leading a better quality of life. Have more drive, be considerate of others, and pursue your dreams.

As a chamber of commerce president for many years, I've listened to more than my share of speakers and have had even more want me to let them speak at my events or for my members. For quite some time, though, when evaluating speakers, I have determined their communicating value by their background, experience, and reasons for speaking. I'm amazed at the number of people who really don't have any motivation other than self-promotion and profitability. They are writing/selling books and speaking because they want to show you how they have made a lot of money selling "it" to others to do the same. Buy my book or come to my talk so I can show you how I used to sleep in a bathtub, couldn't close a sale at a check-out counter, and have no business experience. Still, I can also teach you how to get others to do the same. They were commonly referred to as grifters in the past, but now they are called authors and motivational speakers. I'm sure I'll hear about this paragraph, but this is the point of my book. I want readers to go, "Yeah, wait a minute... hmm??"

Yes, I want to sell some books and have more speaking engagements. Still, I already speak and by invitation on information for businesses, companies, and countries to establish specific industries or methods to succeed. As I stated before, it's for the last 1/3 of my life to leave a legacy and give back from the first two-thirds of my life, not to build wealth on the gullibility and vanity of others.

How about we get started?

1 - WON

I believe most people have heard of a "WIN-WIN" situation. Unfortunately, most people don't know how to reach the WIN-WIN point. Some years ago, I was traveling on a plane going somewhere – a somewhat usual routine for me in my past business experiences. I began thinking of how a particular deal could work. I had to create a winning strategy for both sides, where neither party felt the other was taking advantage. They might realize they had to give up something of value to get something of value. The real trick was what was most valuable to each party regarding the deal.

I asked myself, "What do I need…and what do the others need?" That's when it occurred to me that it was a WIN-WON situation—What I Need – What Others Need.

When planning a business strategy, compromises, negotiations, and resolutions can be reached quickly and efficiently by asking those two viewpoints. Understanding the views is something I will cover in another chapter. What is your primary objective of the transaction, and what is the other party's primary objective? You will know how to maximize meetings and projects when you break those down. On the other hand, you can use the assessment, too, as a method to wear down the opposing side and "win" the deal. Unfortunately, wearing down the opposite side is what some people are all about. It isn't as much about making the deal happen as it is about winning and getting the "better" of the opposing side. Avoid dealing with people like this, as project resolution isn't their main objective. It is just the sport of being the victor.

One can, however, use that assessment to your advantage to ultimately achieve your true objective. If you can begin the negotiations with several things that are irrelevant or secondary to you, knowing that you are ready to give those up to achieve your primary goal. Once again, "What I Need" – objective X. What is it the other needs – to feel as though they won more talking or deal points than you did. Their deals are more about their ego and sport than the actual project. Let them have those, but also be willing to walk away from a project or deal that seems to be about the sport and has no proper resolution. You will realize it wastes your energy and time if you don't, which I will also cover in a later chapter.

To generalize, when engaging in correspondence or communication to accomplish a project, a common assumption is that I want to get this for as little as possible at first review. The opposing party wants to give it to me while getting as much as possible.

This premise applies in almost every interaction, whether in business, personal relationships, or transactions. Decide what you need from the exchange, whether a purchase, a business deal, or a relationship. And consider what they need in return. Are you willing to provide it? Can you provide it? And can you do so ethically or without sacrificing too much in your life or time? Be able to walk away if the return does not fit the investment or expense. And again, that "expense" could be monetary. Still, it could also be time, character, morals, or relationships. These things are much harder to replace or have a much higher value.

A person's true character is seen in times of challenge and failure, not during comfort and success.

2 - TIMING IS EVERYTHING

Time is a commodity that everyone has. It is the most valuable commodity in the world. Unfortunately, we don't know how much time we have. It's like having a checkbook for a checking account but not knowing how much is in the account or when the money will run out.

A few times in my life, I've had to face the reminder time is not promised, nor do we know how much we have or what we have with anyone crucial to us. I have encountered this reality several times in my own life, once with my youngest son, Keller. When he was seven months old, he developed asthma, an attack, and quickly fell ill within 24 hours, which led to a collapsed lung and double pneumonia.

I rushed to a great institution, Texas Children's Hospital, in Houston, where I do not doubt that prayers are responsible for being able to celebrate his

13th birthday recently. Two weeks of a roller coaster of him edging close to death while being connected to thirteen machines daily reminds me of that. One night, the medical team told us Keller would most likely not make it through the night as his organs were starting to shut down. Somebody told his mother and me that he and the child in the room next to him were the sickest in the hospital.

I sat with him and touched him so he could feel me and did the only thing I thought I could do was pray and read the bible out loud with faith it would keep him connected to this world.

That night, the child in the next room passed, and I heard her parents sobbing and just stood by his bed talking to him, wondering if he was following. Morning eventually came, and with the new day, he started to recover. My Father's Day gift that year, a few days later, was getting to hold him out of his crib but still attached to machines.

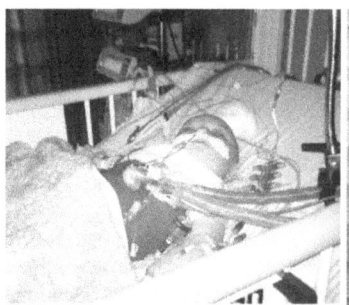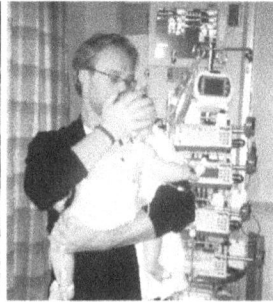

If you do not already, stop now and contemplate and know the value and respect of your time and those around you. Your commodity of time could be increased by spending it on things to improve yourself and value, such as education, experience, time with mentors, etc., but remember, if you don't appreciate your time, no one else will either. Many people will help you waste it, let you freely spend it on their cause, or create their wealth.

How much is your time worth to you and those that love you? Who are you giving or spending that time on? Your time is genuinely all you have to barter with in this life. Value it and the way you spend it. The best thing you can do is invest your time. Invest wisely in people who will appreciate and reciprocate or increase your value and in education, experience, projects, or concepts that will help you to multiply their use and value.

It would help if you also guard your time. Is someone or something stealing it from you? You can make more money, but you can't make more Time. People will guard their money, though, like it is all they have in this world, but they will throw it away or let people steal their commodity of time like it's an endless free resource. When you can learn to manage and control this number one commodity, you are ready to handle the rest of your life. Until then, you will let others take your time, your family, your happiness, and what you value away from you.

From another viewpoint, be the same with other people's time. Have you made them wait because you cannot manage or control your time? Have you treated them like their time is less valuable and easily spent? If you have, you have just taken a portion of that person's life from them. That portion of their life could have gone to their husband/wife, children, and the community, improving their health. You get the picture. As I referred to a time earlier, like a checkbook without knowing the balance – did you write a check for time out of someone else's bank account?

Some years ago, I generously gave my time to many community groups. And they had no problem taking my time; after all, I was giving it away to several organizations. I was given several certificates and awards for this generous time giveaway. It was time I chose to give to their cause and revenue drives, etc., and time I took from my children and wife.

Years later, in the marriage, I was divorced. Not necessarily due to the time away, but I'm sure that didn't help. I remember sitting one afternoon in my office surrounded by paper, wood, and plastic. The awards weren't for just one minute or one action or event but for numerous amounts of time and energy spent on their goals, objectives, and benefits. I was there alone without my children, who were with their mom that weekend. And I remember thinking how much time I had given up and taken from them to give to someone else freely, and I had four walls of plastic, wood, and paper to show for it. The people I valued most and wished to be with were not around. Interestingly, all those people and organizations I had let have those never-to-be-returned portions of my life were not around either.

I'm a firm believer in the idea that we should give back to the community and significantly help those people and organizations in need. However, be discerning about what amount of time and energy you give away and to whom or where it is going. There are ways to do that while sharing the experience with those you love and want to spend time with. Those time capsules can become some of the best memories of time well spent. Evaluate who and what you are giving your time to and from what and whom you are taking the time.

One of the things I developed from that was a time at meals we called Talk-Rock. I went out to the landscaping one evening before dinner, grabbed the first rock I found, and told everyone that whoever had the stone got to talk and ask the others at the table questions. You could only interrupt them or speak out of turn once you held the rock. In the years that followed, this became a great family tradition. We still have that same rock sitting in our kitchen by the meal-time table. Questions used to ask our favorite things about each other, our favorite family vacation, what plans are for summer, etc. The best part is even the youngest children can participate. Their questions are sometimes the best. What animal would you be? What is your favorite game? And other questions that remind you just how simple life used to be.

Our life has different seasons, and we all have them. Sometimes, it's a challenge to switch, but every new season has some great opportunities and adventures if we just let go of the last one. Enjoy the season you are in.

A saying I have and now say to my sons, "I may never come this way again." It is the working title for my second book underway. And what I mean is enjoy wherever you are, whatever you are doing, and whoever you are with because you will never have that same situation again. And you may never go back to experience the place or people you share, good or bad. Be in the "NOW." That is a time well spent.

The commodity of time is doing & having as much control over your time as possible. Paid for your time, you give to someone else for their objectives. What are your objectives? Time is the commodity we all trade with. How much is yours worth? Even when you do a crime, how are you penalized? Being imprisoned removes time from someone's life because that is the most precious commodity. What relationship prisons are you in that may be stealing or wasting your time and energy?

Flash...

They say that your life flashes before your eyes when you die...what will be your flash? I lived my life to be a James Bond movie with so much action that it required an intermission!

3 - TIME OUT

Now that you are hopefully looking at the importance of your time, its value, and to use it as your commodity of life and its use and management of what will ultimately be your happiness, success, and legacy, let's break it down into perspective.

I've seen several combinations of time allotments with catchy spins or rhymes. Still, I've always looked at them, thinking, what world are they living in?

My principles of time have been relatively simple, so I'm passing those along to you again with the WIN-WON philosophy (What I need/What Others Need) In that schematic, dividing your time into six -4 hour areas is more practical and feasible. Let me break it down:

<u>6-4's</u>

1- 4 hours of quality sleep

2- 4 hours of flex time used for extra rest, commuting, meals, or borrowed to expand productivity/work

3- 4 hours of productivity/work in the morning

4- 4 hours of productivity/work in the afternoon

5- 4 hours of flex time used for commuting, meals, or borrowed from to expand productivity/work

6- 4 hours for personal use and quality of life

We are breaking our lives down into allotments of four hours. We use four hours for quality sleep and flex time, as I call it, to get more sleep, commute, or transition at the start of the day. Four hours for productivity/ work in the morning; four hours of productivity/work in the afternoon; four hours of flex/transition time used in the afternoon to complete work, commute, and transition into our evening; and four hours for yourself/your interests. The time allotments may not flow as smoothly as that, but they usually follow that structure.

Unfortunately, the time we usually rob is four hours for ourselves in personal use and quality of life.

I usually only get 4-6 hours of sleep, and many highly successful people I know are the same way.

This concept of 8-10 hours may have been great when I was eight or for the sleeping aid commercials. Still, realistically, most people don't achieve that. Suppose you can optimize your sleep and get the targeted eight hours, which is good for you. I've found that this is the time area sacrificed when special occasions pop up or work late. So, I will leave it up to the reader to determine how their four-hour increments best fit their lifestyle and what is feasible.

And although we have a supposed 8-hour workday, you are doing great if you can get a solid 6 hours of productivity. The Third allotment of four hours is significant, though - think about it. Sometimes, if you do sleep over or sometimes, if you do work longer, it comes from a pool of hours that are transitional.
Commuting to and from work or projects, activities, kids' activities, extended work lunches, coffee breaks, and bathroom breaks is the flexible pool of hours used wherever the day or week may change or require adaptation of your time for work, sleep, and transitions.

And when you aren't working, such as on weekends, holidays, or vacations, you get the productive four-hour allotments restored to your pool of hours for use. The four hours of flex time apply to breakfast, lunch, dinner, driving, and similar transitional daily life activities. Although it is not necessarily a productive time in our lives, it is necessary to get to the other allotments of the four that are.

The final four hours I'm talking about are for you to use for the quality of life and essential memories such as prayer, meditation, health, family time, self-improvement, reading, and other activities that provide quality of life, health, and mental revitalization.

It would help if you were stingy, giving these four hours to the other pools of time. Four hours or less of your time/life should at least be yours to determine. If you do the math, that is under 20% of your time for your time.

You are utilizing One-third of your time for sleep, meals, and body maintenance and another third spent on productivity/work. Approximately 16% of the time, you flex and use varying daily depending upon the needs and demands of family and work. You must use your four hours impactfully and strategically to improve and enhance yourself and your life. Not just for yourself, but by doing so, it will also impact and improve your relationships and quality with others.

You should draft a daily schedule to start. Just use blocks for sleep and work - they are a given. Think about maximizing your four-hour flex and transition periods, one in the morning and one in the afternoon. Then, take your time and seriously consider how you would use four hours a day for YOU.
Exercise, reading, meditation, quality-focused time with family, significant others, children, parents, friends, and others of value.

Try to detail and realize how important these four hours are in your life and how you can make them quality and investment into what matters most. Your close relationships, health, education, rest/relaxation, memorable moments, and events – the "Be in the Now" time.

Another essential aspect to consider as you evaluate your daily use of time is giving yourself grace and permission to let the past be the past. Maybe you haven't done the things you would like or as much as you would like up to this point but move forward. Don't let yourself or anyone else recall your past like it determines your future. If that happens, you must reassess your time with that individual, group, activity, or organization and decrease it or give them none. I will address that in the Quicksand chapter.

I am blessed to have opportunities, and note I refer to them as opportunities, not jobs, that I got to travel, see the world, and determine a lot of my time. I have tried to go places, see things, and do things constantly and not wait for a holiday, a long weekend, two weeks of vacation a year, or retirement. I wanted to do and experience some things early in life so that if I waited for retirement, I might need more physical ability, health, or energy. That's if I even lived to retirement. As I have written, we do not know how much time is spent in our time checking accounts. It could run out in a few years, months, weeks, or days.

I am saddened when I talk to people, and they keep referring to their life plan as being all about a magical retirement that they may never see. When they arrive, they will have missed many opportunities or places that will no longer be accessible or viable to experience. Don't get me wrong, you should make your life plan to save and allow for life in its last third, but don't treat it like this satisfying and fulfilling utopia. In my opinion, life would be better spent in retirement, being able to tell your stories about a life of experiences and travel to children, grandchildren, and friends. Or to re-visit places of memories and take others to show them the excitement of what you already know.

This planning also allows for periods in life where finances may be less or minimal and even sometimes directed toward unexpected medical costs or life events. You may need to be more conservative with funds. If you wait all your life to get to that magic utopia of retirement to travel and "live," what happens if unplanned life events, tragedy, or health drain funds, and none of those unforgettable trips and moments never get to happen? There is no do-over button.

After this chapter:

1. Stop, put the book down, and do something to symbolize a new start.
2. Walk, meditate, pray, talk to a confidant, or do something ceremonial to mark a new beginning.
3. Whatever will mentally impact a fresh start, write in this book below the date and time you made a new start of owning YOUR time.

Today begins a new ownership of my life and my time, and it began: _____

Success isn't working all year to enjoy two weeks – Success is living a life you enjoy every day.

4 – US VS THEM

Today's environment for consumers and businesses never ceases to amaze me. Again, with the two sides of What I Need and What Others Need, you have the consumer and business sides. The consumer needs good value, treatment, appreciation, and respect. The business needs good product quality, loyal consumers/clients, valued and quality employees, and reasonable profit to operate and be successful and respected.

Over the years, though, instead of what used to be almost a competition with the type of customer service consumers would receive, it has now turned into what seems like a Us versus Them scenario. Do you think of consumers as customers and clients, or are they victims and targets? When your attitude and policies reflect ways to "trick" or take advantage of your customers, you should rethink your business or company culture.

Here are some examples of some of the declines and irritations I noticed. Depending on whatever side of the transaction you're on, I hope you will consider the other side and bring everyone back to the "respected" position.

When I order food, coffee, etc., frequently, have you noticed this fantastic trend of asking you to select your "tip" upfront? And anymore it starts at 18% and goes up to as high as 30%. Now, the agreed wait staff relies upon and deserves a generous supplement to their meager hourly wage, but to ask for it before I even received any service is a bit much. You still need to show me the type of service I will receive to know what to tip you. An additional issue is the tip awaiting at checkout. So, because you put in my order and took my money, which was so above the call of duty, should you receive a 20% commission because you showed up for work with a pulse?

I like to be a generous tipper, but I also want to incentivize the wait staff for the type of service I'm receiving. Supporting the old principle, you will get rewarded for hard work. Today's tipping culture is apparently if the wait staff could walk to my table, a 20% premium better slap on the table.

It's the everyone-gets-a-trophy carried into adult years. Further irritation happens when I'm paying in cash. Instead of returning change to provide a tip variation or handing me a big bill, I guess they either assume they were so awful they only deserve a couple of dollars and some change or a 40% premium by leaving the $ 20's or $50 on the table. I will likely still make the appropriate tip from other change in my wallet, or I might even ask them to return with one of the bills broken into minor currency to tag the percent warranted accurately. But, on a few occasions, when I've even had to get up and find a pitcher to fill my water, I go, "OK… you're right. You do only deserve the few bills and change you brought me."

So, as a waitperson, do the consumer a favor and return with appropriate nominations to tip appropriately, or don't get mad for getting what you truly deserve. And don't get upset if you think because the very fact that you showed up for work constitutes a monetary trophy. In that case, the waitperson or business owner should display gratitude to the consumer for showing up to you and being a loyal customer who could have supported a competitor with our money and patronage instead of being ungrateful and smirking.

On the other hand, as a consumer, this person isn't a family member or your concierge. They are probably in a position like that due to scheduling flexibility as an income supplement or because they are pursuing college and other endeavors to improve their life. They, too, have a family, and your tips could determine that person's daily needs, such as the gas to get home to their family that night. The final amount needed is to make enough to pay rent or provide groceries at home for their little ones similar to the ones you have sitting beside you.

Consider how you want your son, daughter, mother, sister, brother, or father treated in this situation.

Because you know what, they are exactly that to someone. And it's not funny or tasteful to joke about how poorly you responded to that person and their attempt to wait on you and let you enjoy and focus on the time with your family, business colleagues, or memorable moments. I hate when I see someone at another table act that way. Still, I usually project that's probably how they live with all their relationships and transactions, un-evenly sided in the give-receive life dynamic. If you are like this, I'll tell you that others besides me sitting at a distant table have noticed, and it's probably keeping some opportunities and relationships away or distant from you.

I've flown to every state and nearly 60 countries worldwide numerous times. In doing so, I have traveled on about 70 airlines. Some of which are no longer even around. I keep track of them and recall and tell others about my experiences – which probably supports the "some of which are no longer around" statement, not because of my single incident, but due to many consumers having a similar experience and now, like me, choosing another airline.

I will give a few examples but leave out the airline's names. I want to provide some real-life experiences, but I will use something other than this medium, as a bully pulpit or a vehicle, to get even. I want this book to help everyone on either side of the WIN-WON dynamic. Giving examples is a better way to do it rather than shaming or getting even.

I will admit, though, in person, when I talk to people, I do tell the airlines, businesses, or organizations' names because I think in my role, I must inform or at least prepare family, friends, clients, and members to expectations or experiences and look out for their interests.

I was flying back from Los Angeles a few years ago after attending a movie premier red-carpet event.

I am very gracious to be invited and to have gotten to attend. So, I'm in a good mood and even excited to return to Houston, where I live. I had booked an airline considered an economy airline, but the flight time and price were perfect for what I needed. My companion and I were there and ready to leave at midday. Well, the flight got the dreaded "delayed" tag. OK, no problem, I'm in a good mood; I've traveled and experienced this many times. I am just going to enjoy one of the lounges.

The new flight time finally arrived, and then again delayed. OK, once again, I won't let it ruin this fantastic trip and life experience, so I just returned to the lounge. But this time, I started checking the weather and other circumstances that may be causing the continued delay. I've noticed no other airline is having delays, especially none also going to Houston. No cloud is in the sky between Los Angeles and Houston, so this airline's internal issues must be staffing, maintenance, or connection delays.

I'm checking because if it's weather-related, you're on your own. However, if it's the airline's problem, the airline must meet certain obligations to its passengers. The other issue is that we are now getting into the night, and there are fewer and fewer flights available if I want to switch and still get home on the same day. I'm starting to get suspicious. As a seasoned traveler, I book a hotel nearby if I'm stranded another day. I'm all proud of myself and my ability to have lounge service and a waiting room nearby. If this goes south, there are 200+ passengers they will have to house for the night. I can imagine what might be left nearby or the type of accommodation we might get stuck in at midnight.

Well, we head to the gate, and at this point, it's late, and no other flights are taking off to Houston if this one doesn't go. As I suspected, they finally announced it was a canceled flight, and the passengers would be rescheduled for a flight the following day. There was a unison moan that echoed throughout the LAX terminal.

Now, I noticed my fellow passengers at each reorganizing effort of the two original times to leave. Usually, on a discounted airline, if you've done a lot of flying, you know people and families are probably living close to the edge and paycheck to paycheck. I had observed several moms traveling with children, especially one Hispanic mother with three children, probably all under age six – one a few months old. She had been keeping them with food at airport prices all day and had perhaps exhausted traveling funds. I saw several elderly and an older Asian couple who didn't speak English. My heart sank. I got this sudden protective pride that these were my fellow Houstonians, and this wouldn't go down this way.

I knew the airline needed to provide hotel accommodations and food vouchers. Still, I also realized the airline had not announced that, and I bet most of these people didn't know that. The airline had not mentioned that in the announcement, so I approached the counter and asked the airline employee if she would announce that. She looked at me with a bit of concern and made a vague announcement that if they went to customer service at another location in the terminal, they could speak to a customer service representative. Again, they should have disclosed what that event meant or what they would be seeing the customer service representative and what to expect.

Well, anyone who knows me knows I can be bold at times. Because I've spoken in public numerous times, I am OK with instantly taking over a big crowd or getting noticed. So, I had one of my moments, as my sons refer to it, "Oh no, there goes Dad" moments, and from the counter, speaking loudly. Without using a microphone, I announced who I was as a chamber president of the Houston Intercontinental airport area. This airline, by regulations, owed all of them hotel accommodations and food vouchers if they wanted them. I looked back at the airline representative, and she was like a deer in headlights. She quickly commented OK, but they all had to go to the customer service area in the other part of the terminal. I responded, we both know you hope that most of these people will give up, not find it, or let me guess, there will be one representative there, and this will take hours.

I told her we were leaving the gate area when you or a representative walked them to the counter so they could find it and assist them. I then turned to the group and said no one would leave this gate until they came to take you to customer service; they were hoping you would give up or wouldn't find it. With total disgust, she got on the phone and called someone. Within a few minutes, a jacketed representative showed up, and we began our pilgrimage of over 200 passengers walking together, filling the hall of the terminal as we walked together and helping each other to customer service. But wait, it gets better.

Upon our arrival, the airline had only two customer service representatives waiting. The passengers began receiving hotel assignments and were given a few hotel vouchers. People started showing me the vouchers but needed to figure out how to get to their assigned hotel. A couple of people got put in a hotel room together and didn't know each other. And they had no food vouchers.

Again, my blood started to boil, so I went to the counter. I asked the airline customer service representatives, "So, are you busing everyone to these hotels because they are not nearby?
And where are their food vouchers? I started pointing to small children and older adults and saying you've had them here since noon and no food. They need to

eat. Again, with disgust and spite, the customer service representative looked at me, said just a moment, and got on the phone.

She called the airport police, and everything stopped. I thought, well, this is getting good, and thinking, well, at the very least, I'll not be allowed on this airline again, but my hotel accommodations tonight might be in a cell snuggled up to a big guy named Butch.

Three officers arrived and pulled me aside. I showed them my identification, explained the situation, and showed them a few pictures on my phone that further demonstrated my background and genuine intention. They smiled, stepped back, looked at the representative, leaned against the wall, and said, "He's good." The look of disbelief and terror on the representative's face would have made a great commercial for Mastercard; it's a priceless ad.

I then approached her and said, now it's my turn. I'm calling (I gave a person's name I know at an LA TV station) and having them send over a news crew. I'm having those people (pointing to an elderly couple and a mom with three kids, stand behind me when they interview me. And I've called my staff, and they are setting up a meeting for me with the Los Angeles mayor and Chamber of Commerce president. Tomorrow, I'm contacting (a gentleman I knew of at the FAA from a project I had helped with at one of my member airlines). I'll begin filing complaints with a few hundred passengers. I can be an ass at times. I did call the TV station and was going to call the guy at the FAA, but I wasn't going to bother the mayor or a peer at the area chamber.

I just wanted her to start thinking of the fallout from not doing what she knew they should do.

With that revelation, within a few minutes, additional representatives showed up. The passengers were finally getting what they deserved. Moms hugged me, even cried, showed me how they were staying at the nearby Hilton or Sheraton, and had food vouchers because, you see, the nearby hotels all had shuttle service. The bus service would have been a logistics nightmare if they had not booked hotels with shuttles.

I was also called back to the counter and offered my hotel room and vouchers so I could be on my way, and they could get rid of me. But to their chagrin, I informed them I would be the last person to leave after I knew everyone on the flight was accommodated and had hotel or food vouchers. I went to the hotel I had previously booked. After all of that, the person and I later laughed because, in the end, I was the only passenger who paid for a room for the night. My hotel was less pleasant of a hotel than most of the passengers had received. But wait, there's more…

So, the following day, I arrived and was back at the airport. I swear it was like Christmas morning, and I was Dad. All these passengers came up to me and thanked me. Moms had little kids hugging me and telling me about the hotel they stayed at, and they had never stayed in anything of this level before. It was one of the most incredible moments, as I say, "Some days it's good to be me."

Having become this group's tour guide, I waited until every passenger boarded and boarded the plane myself. When I stepped onto it and started walking from the front of the aircraft to the aisle, the passengers applauded me. It was one of the most genuine applauses I've ever gotten.

We sit there, and everyone seems happy and talking as the event creates camaraderie amongst the passengers. Then, an announcement came that we would be a little late pulling out of the gate.

Someone yelled a long, slow "REGGIE," and the plane burst into laughter. I had to respond, yelling out, "Guys, sorry, but I can't fly the plane."

Eventually, we arrived in Houston and went down to the baggage carousel. Thankful fathers greeted me, children of elderly grandparents, husbands, and spouses, all having heard about me, I guess, from those stranded. I was getting thanked, and people were taking pictures with me, getting my email address and contact information. That was another incredible moment.

And then one last occurrence. We were waiting for our luggage, and it had been a long wait when an announcement or word had circulated regarding a luggage delay. Once again, that long, loud "REGGIE" was yelled out. The crowd laughed again, but I thought all right, why not? So, I went to the baggage customer service area. The representative informed me it was raining extremely hard. They had delayed getting the luggage off the plane a little, and OK, that seemed reasonable. Well, I did absolutely nothing, but I kid you not; the minute I walked back to the carousel, the light went off, and the baggage started spitting out onto the conveyor. The crowd once again broke out into applause.

After that, I quickly grabbed my bag and told the person I had been traveling with to get out of there, or they would ask and expect me to stop the rain. That was a great memory and a significant example of how NOT to execute good customer service.

Unfortunately, I have other stories involving airlines and poor customer service. Still, many people have those, and I've made my point. Treat customers how you want to be treated as a customer and remember they are moms, children, grandparents, and family members. How would you like the ones you care about treated?

My final overview for this topic is to break down quite simply. We are all just people. A company isn't this innate object of an unfeeling, uncaring mass that survives to generate profits at the expense of unsuspecting and gullible human beings. It's other people making a living for their families with daily issues and challenges. Treat each interaction with the principle of What I Need (consideration, patience, thoughtfulness, and respect) with What Others Need (consideration, patience, thoughtfulness, and respect).

Do Unto Others as You Would Have Them Do Unto YOU.

5 - VIEWPOINT

When making decisions and considering both sides of a situation, it boils down to the person's or organization's viewpoint. How are you looking at the situation or issue? What is its value to you or the other side? What is the background of how you got to this interface? What are the experiences of those influencing the outcome? What motivates them?

These questions are for you to consider as you begin the process, or at least right before you decide to impact the process. Are you the solution to the problem(s), or are you the problem?

When I hire someone, it is because I need a problem solved. Make sure you don't hire people that just become another problem for you to resolve.

Many people also use problems (excuses) not to complete tasks or projects. Excuses like not enough training, not enough information, not enough assistance, or whatever rationalizes non-performance. One can always find reasons and ways not to succeed, but employers and leaders like those who look for ways to overcome problems.

Be tolerant of others' views. Don't even say I disagree with them; they are their rights, but they stop when there is any force, verbally or physically, to express or apply yours to others. Your rights have stepped over their boundaries into someone else's. You have yours; they have theirs. The view of accepting people, regardless of religion, sexual preference, etc., should be something we all aspire to achieve. It's above my pay grade to judge people.

Politics and religion are two topics that can make a conversation go south quickly. There is no reason to avoid either one. The problem only arises when one or more people's viewpoints are overstated or too aggressive and disregard the rights of others in the conversation or forum. Suppose your perspective requires a loud or bold assertion to be conveyed; then it's weak in substance and must result in bullying, or shock and awe to have any impact.

Religion, to some, is like a raincoat. Their faith and judgment are worn when it's raining or hard times, but when it's sunny, they take it off. Their religion somehow to them, justifies acting elite to others.

Do your viewpoints come with validity or experience, or are they shallow and must be supplemented by aggressive methods, quips, or insults? If they have a reasonable balance, they will be considered or embraced; if not, remember it is still the right of the other person, and their experiences are different from yours, so their views probably are too.

A good example I will detail is an ongoing challenge my ex-wife and I faced regarding raising sons. She is a remarkable and brilliant woman but an only child with little interaction with the male world. I suggest one approach, and she would tell another on many occasions. Our views were motivated as such – mine I kept insisting I wanted to raise alpha males who would lead, protect, and provide. She was trying to mold them into how women would like men to be.

My counter was always, hey, if we had a girl, you got me; I would defer to you because I do not know or understand what it's like to be in a woman's world. I can understand, listen, and respond to requests or traits that women find attractive in a man, but I can't be there mentally, and I'm ok with that. Although boys need to learn how to be considerate and thoughtful toward girls/women to try to understand them and treat and refer to them as equals with the same or greater respect. Women also need to consider that men must operate in a man's world with other men that sometimes are not what women molded or would prefer them to be. And although some things are getting better and we have come a long way for women's equality, we can do better.

But give men some grace; sometimes we must influence the old school, and yes, perhaps outdated males still in existence and we as men must interface with them. If males don't interface as boys or men, they are left to the side and usually treated as outsiders. It's a fine line, and boys, as they are shaping their character like young ladies do, can be caught in between worlds, and feel stranded without other fellow guys' support and camaraderie or teammates.

A good example I heard was in a couple's retreat, where they explained how men and women communicate with peers differently. Women talk to each other face to face and share and usually expand, expressing not just the issue but their emotions and feelings regarding the problems.

Men, however, communicate by sitting side by side in a setting such as watching a game, fishing, hunting, etc. We will sit side by side as a peer and an ally facing whatever. Let's talk about the issue or say it out loud. I'm not expecting the other guy to fix it; listen to it.

In transition to the next point - men are programmed to fix things. So, when women talk to men about their issues, we feel we need to fix it. But women often don't want us to fix it; they want us to hear and share with them.

At the retreat, a few couples taught it. One couple had been married for almost 30 years. They had been high school sweethearts; the husband had worked for one company all his life, and she had stayed home all her life to raise the family and care for the household. They, at one point, referred to themselves as vanilla ice cream. Because although it didn't have a lot of toppings or frills, it was sweet and enjoyable. That's what they were trying to say.

Another couple that was teaching had both been divorced before and had a mixed family, as it is now called, with children from previous marriages. They had encountered ex-spouses, children adjusting, and moving to a new home; both had careers and several other modern-day challenges.

Now, in my opinion, staying in a marriage for 30 years is impressive and not easy; however, when asked about the couple I wanted to sit through an afternoon session with, I responded that while they were like vanilla ice cream, I and my life was more like a banana split with a lot of toppings, knocked off the table. Now I needed to scoop it back up, get into the banana boat cup, and not just make it look edible but somehow delicious. I wanted to hear from the dysfunctional couple. They get me. It's all from the viewpoint.

My last viewpoint comes from a recent US Global Leadership Coalition lunch. We discussed global policies with various topics and countries that are top of the news, such as China, Russia, Ukraine, Israel, and Iran. We shared viewpoints on the countries, trade, policy, etc. These types of settings and topics provide various views economically and politically. One comment made, though, gave me a "Hmmm?" moment. Suppose green energy is so efficient and practical. Why isn't China, which manufactures most of the products for these industries? Why are they still the biggest user of fossil fuels? And why is the US spending so much on it while China continues to use the cheaper and more accessible approach to energy? These questions are something to consider.

You can always find excuses not to succeed, but those who do succeed look for solutions to the excuses.

6 – COMMUNICATION IS KEY

Speak to and communicate with others how you would want to be shared/treated. Or as you would wish someone you care about to be treated. Show respect and admiration, which can carry a lot of value when negotiating.

I must admit I have been forceful and strong or opinionated at times, but luckily, I have learned to stop and ask myself, is this how I hope they speak to me or worse, is this how I would want someone speaking or communicating with my family, kids, or employees? Have I overstepped my bounds to show how "good" I am at giving someone a tongue laceration, as I call it? What is the objective here? Is it to communicate and accomplish a goal, or are personalities at play clashing to show dominance or arrogance? Are you listening to understand so you can communicate better, or are you just listening for your next opportunity to talk?

We had a small acreage with a cabin called the Lazy G Ranch. We had purchased it, and I used the opportunity to teach my sons various skills like building walls, plumbing, flooring, sheetrock, and other useful traits. It also gave them an incredible feeling of accomplishment and ownership. But one of my favorite things was getting up each morning while everyone else was sleeping, making my morning coffee, and sitting on the porch with my tin coffee cup. My middle son, Royce, keeps it to this day as one of his best memories of me at the ranch.

Those mornings were some of my "take time to smell the roses" moments. I recall some great moments with my sons, Remington, Royce, and Keller, as babies and small boys. I would listen to nature awaken, watch the wind through the tops of the trees, and observe how nature communicated. It was very therapeutic for me. I noticed birds would communicate and await a response; the wind would flow from one tree to the next until it reached me. I got to feel what I had to witness the trees enjoy until it was my turn, and it caught me. Occasionally, there might be a gunshot in the distance during hunting season, or a loud plane or helicopter fly over, and the animals would go quiet and still. Then, eventually, everything would start again back in its harmony. One morning, I had an epiphany that was an excellent example of how to communicate and some of the examples of how we do things wrong.

It is how you communicate like nature, where it sounds off and awaits another to talk. Or you can see the breeze coming, but you must wait your turn to enjoy and experience what you see others experiencing. Or are you the gunshot or loud plane, all artificial I took note of, that disturbs the natural process? It makes everything else stop because it doesn't sound natural. It disrupts the flow of everyone else and their ability to contribute.

Yes, I know how very Zen of me. Maybe it was the result of getting up too early or too much coffee, but after I realized that every morning for the months that followed, it was a similar pattern. Ask yourself, how do you communicate with those around you? Superiors, subordinates, peers, friends, your family.

Stop and make a list of three ways you could communicate better, and more importantly, make a list of those around you that you would like to make a better effort to communicate, which means listening AND speaking.

Another habit I learned early in business, sitting on multiple boards or having to attend committee or project meetings, was when I was new to the group, or there were unique personalities to join the group, take time to sit still and listen and observe. Watch the dynamics between people. See who is respected and maybe who is just tolerated. Identify the leaders of the subgroups or committees and show them respect or watch what makes them tick or respond positively.

Learn their needs to better express or obtain your needs from the group. You can make them allies, and respectful peers or you can make them antagonists, and they may disregard your objectives, not even because they are bad ideas but because they came from you. Yes, it is counter-productive, but I've witnessed it happen many times.

I have learned how to control or gain the attention or camaraderie of strangers by identifying the sub-group leader and gaining their friendship or trust, allowing myself to achieve the group's support without having

to win over everyone. Getting the leaders' support can be as simple as playing to their ego or subtly identifying them as leaders or something special in the group.

On one of my trips to Europe, I was in Rome for a few days. I had an evening and wanted to watch some sports on TV. I found a Scottish pub/restaurant near the city center just a couple miles from the Coliseum.

I ordered dinner and watched the game while enjoying it. I found it humorous that I had located an English (Scottish dialect) pub in Rome where I could talk to people since I speak very little Italian. While engaging different people, I distinctly heard two other American accents.

The two other gentlemen and I quickly bonded due to the American connection, and they both turned out to be remarkable gentlemen. One was a National Geographic photographer, and the other was his long-time friend, a New York Times journalist with impressive careers and adventures.

We talked and exchanged travel adventures and stories but soon decided it was time to adventure out into Rome, true to all three of our natures. They wanted to take me to a popular restaurant and club where we could walk to catch the flavor of Rome.

Upon arrival, we headed upstairs to the balcony that overlooked the entire establishment and where more of the dining took place, while the bottom floor was for mixing and much more of a standing-only area. We positioned ourselves so we could people-watch and take in the atmosphere. They were making comments and observations about different groups and people. Not in a derogatory manner, but who was in charge, their possible stories, background, and reason for being there. In a group, you can tell the leader, because they are usually centered, and everyone's positioned toward them. They are usually the more charismatic and have obvious traits or characteristics that stand out and identify why others probably defer to them.

So, having tested this exercise a few other times successfully, I told them I bet I could "take over" the place in under 30 minutes. They remarked that I said I had not been here before and hadn't come to Rome but maybe once a year. How did I plan on doing that if I didn't know anyone? I asked them for a wager that they would have to pick up the check if I could do it. Of course, it was on. They ordered heavily after that certain I was paying.

I asked our waitress to come over and asked if she had worked there long. She had, so she was perfect for my sociology exercise. I wanted an established employee that the regulars would already know and identify. I then gave her a budget of $100 for specials on the menu, such as drinks, desserts, etc.

Load up a tray with them and then come back to me.

In about 15 minutes, she arrived loaded with rewards. Then I informed her that I wanted her to go to different tables or groups she knew that were regulars or popular, and give or let the "leader" of the group, whom I would identify or point out, pick something from the tray. She was to point to me and say it's compliments of the Texan.

Now, a little note here. I was born and originated in Missouri but have spent most of my life in Texas. So, when I introduced myself, I say I'm from Texas. I found that when traveling abroad, people may or may not like Americans, depending upon where you are. Still, for some reason, almost everyone likes Texans. There is this stereotype or mysticism internationally about Texans. We all wear boots and hats and ride horses; most of the time, they think we are packing a gun. They usually light up with questions or stand back in respect or fear. I don't know which.

Now, back to the tray-toting ambassador. She started on the balcony where we were sitting and began going to tables and doing as I asked. The person that I identified always lit up and beamed with pride.

They were exceptional and recognized as worthy of the Texan's flattery. The waitress and tray continued downstairs. I quickly started watching as those on the floors made thankful gestures to me by lifting their drinks, waving their hands, or even yelling "To the Texan" in Italian-English accent.

Patrons watched in anticipation of being singled out in their crowd as deserving of special treatment. People started reciprocating and sending us things and even came to meet us and flooded the table. People were taking pictures with me, and I was the talk of the club in under 30 minutes. My night's expenses were free.

My two newly established friends were amazed and had one of their most remarkable nights ever in Rome. I have once again made the point I am stressing in this chapter. Identify the leaders of the group and align with them. With your objectives met, others will become your champions to be a part of the dynamics.

Identifying and aligning with leaders will give you synergies and dynamics that motivate others to champion your causes and objectives.

7 – QUICKSAND

As you go through this book and evaluate the two sides of a deal, relationship, transaction, or engagement – the What I Need/What Others Need concept, there is a particular area I want to focus on and refer to as "QUICKSAND."

Growing up in a family with many ministers, I, and most of my family, have a very giving or serving mentality. The role I have had for many years as a chamber president fits my personality well. However, with that, it has also had consequences.

My role is to assist people and businesses with problems or issues. This need to constantly save or fix problems has left me with an easy target on my head to be taken advantage of. In your life, you need to be careful of relationships or situations that can result in a person or company being in "quicksand" and you wanting or trying to pull them out.

You may want or need to have this feeling of saving or fixing a problem, whether for a person, a business, a situation, or a relationship, but what do they need? What are they trying to get out of the engagement? Are they looking for resolution, assistance, improvement, or advancement? Or will you be another person they will take advantage of because their moral or credibility checkbook is empty?

I've had people try to use my contacts or credible situations to benefit them a few times because theirs was exhausted or ruined. They may utilize your favors or position to help them, leaving you the bill or the consequences when they burn that opportunity.

Sometimes, they will pull you into the quicksand with them. And what's worse is that when you realize it, hopefully in time, and decide to get out of the situation before being pulled under, too, they will execute repercussions on you for leaving them in the quicksand. They may even mentally justify anything they do to impact you or those around you for doing so. How dare you save yourself and not go along with their plan.

If you ask someone who knows me, I tell people to prepare. They either like me or they don't. But I tell them if you dig deeper, you usually find that they don't like me because I didn't do what they wanted or fall into their plan or scheme. I probably even removed myself from the situation or relationship. I advise you to do the same.

Be careful of these types of people and situations. They are toxic and can do more damage to you and even those around you. It can damage your ability to help or impact others who will really need, appreciate, value, and benefit from your assistance. Deal with these people or situations by keeping a distance or giving them the information that can assist them but limit your participation or denote to those involved your limited involvement or ties to them. You can't save everyone or every situation, and it's ok not to try.

At this point, stop and ask yourself – am I in any toxic relationships or situations, and am I in quicksand?
Put the book down, list those people or situations, and evaluate how to minimize the damage or exit altogether. I will warn you now: it may not be easy and may take several steps or time, but in the long run, it's your life, and I've already emphasized we have limited time, and you need to control your use and outcome.

YOU can't change a toxic person or situation, but you can CHANGE how much time and energy you let them take from you.

8 – IT'S PERSONAL

Most people have heard about the "Golden Rule," which means treating others as you want them to treat you. Well, I beg to defer a little bit. Once again, the Win-Won Rule applies here too. Sometimes, you shouldn't treat people the way YOU want (What I Need) but treat them the way THEY want (What Others Need). You, for example, may want to be quiet and reserved and relax at parties. They, however, may need the attention and admiration of others. They may need to feel as though they are the center of attention.

This reference reminds me of another of my favorite cliché – People may not remember what you said, but they will remember how you made them feel. I think this is very true. I have witnessed people at high school reunions or running into old friends or past boyfriends/ girlfriends. Their very personality will morph back into this "former self" due to the way that person made them feel about themselves.

Keep yourself focused on what you have become or the route to becoming, not on your past or past failures. It is important to remember where you come from and how far you have come, not to remind you of past demons but to celebrate your accomplishments. Use it for fuel to give you confidence and encouragement from the inside. Recall it not to bring you down but to only further validate you have earned the right and the grace of God to be where you are or want to be.

Use this also to provide tolerance and understanding for others and those you wish to interact with or engage in a deal, transaction, or relationship. Put yourself in their shoes to better understand their motivations, objectives, and goals. This mental view will help you to determine their viewpoint, as was written about earlier.

I often wear gray suits when meeting new people or at mixer events. The reason is some people use visual associations to remember you. I try to use the gray suit to give them a color/visual association with my name – Gray. Maybe you can find a unique characteristic, feature, or item that helps you stand out or gives others an excellent visual association memory to associate with you.

I've known people who like to wear hats, a specific elaborate piece of jewelry, or a pen. It's not that your outfit or items need to be bedazzled, but it may help others to remember you and stand apart from others.

Another note is I usually make it a rule to dress up or dress above the situation or event. It is another cliché, but it is better to be overdressed than underdressed. I've always thought I'm not dressing up for myself but to show the person I'm going to meet I value them and the meeting. That person was worth dressing up and looking my best.

I received a nice compliment once about what I've accomplished and how I helped or inspired them. I responded that I'd hit more foul balls than home runs, but I kept swinging. And although home runs are what show up on the scoreboard, it's ok to hit fouls because if you do, you get another pitch.

Keep swinging at your objectives and projects. And just like a good coach should tell you – more than anything, enjoy yourself – it's just a game.

When you get opportunities to attend events or be in places that provide new introductions or life experiences, you must capitalize on them and take advantage of them. I had some great opportunities a few times in my life, and I let others prevent them from happening. Years ago, I decided not to let other people influence or prevent good opportunities from happening to me because of that. Is there someone or something in your life that makes you hesitate to take or act on good opportunities for business, travel, life experiences, meetings, personal introductions, or personalities? They may be preventing you from reaching your full potential.

If they genuinely were a companion, friend, or supporter, they would encourage you and be excited or at least happy about that opportunity for you. Unfortunately, others I've spoken to about these situations usually say later that a person isn't even in their life anymore due to that type of personality, and they rob them of that chance. When this happens, remind them they should be supportive and excited for you.

Remember the principle here: What I Need, What Others Need. You should take advantage of this opportunity or life experience. However, they need to feel more important and still of value in your life if they are not allowed this same experience. Please don't use a situation to manipulate or take advantage of someone who cares about you because it may jeopardize the values and trust you have established with each other.

I've been very blessed and met several US Presidents back to George Bush and many foreign Presidents, Prime ministers, and royalty. I don't have pictures of some of my most extraordinary events because, as I say, if you were taking pictures – you didn't belong there. It was a rare occasion for you, and you had better capture it, or no one would believe you. For example, almost all my meetings with US Presidents except for President Trump – where I made the Fox News televised event, were at private or smaller gatherings such as at a home or special event. A couple of the most unique events involved former President of Mexico, Vicente Fox, and in the Middle East with the Prince of Bahrain.

However, one opportunity that I regret and let another influence and stop me was an opportunity to meet the Queen of England. The Queen would travel to Malta and host an annual British Commonwealth event. The Queen would travel on what many felt would be one of her last trips out of the UK, which proved accurate. There was to be an annual polo match between the Queen's Guard and the Malta Polo Club, the oldest polo club in Europe.

This event would have a VIP area and reception for a few selected guests. Since I had helped the country with some projects, even planning the event, and had established a good rapport with the Prime Minister at the time, Joesph Muscat, I would have the opportunity to be in the area with her. However, for the event planned on or near the US holiday of Thanksgiving, I would have to either be away from my family for the holiday or bring them to Malta. Unfortunately, they could also not be in the area with me. They could attend the match and everything else. Still, the area had a limited capacity, and too many others would be given the honor with the Queen. When I expressed this to my wife at the time, I got an earful. So, to avoid further discourse, I dropped the trip altogether.

I never got the opportunity to meet her again. I did, however, later get a chance to meet with Sarah, the Duchess of York, and discuss the event and other things.

Don't let others discourage you, and don't be the one to deter or stand in the way of opportunities, life experiences, and benefits to those you care about around you. Take advantage of your opportunities, introductions, and meetings, and realize they can pop up anytime. You never know who's watching or when you might meet them again. Opportunities open doorways for you.

Meetings pictured include Sarah the Duchess of York (Fergie) and former Prime Minister of Malta, Joesph Muscat.

Doorways…
Many things happen in the doorways. We make decisions to enter – we make decisions to leave. We may have our first kiss – we may say goodbye. Sometimes, we open the doors – sometimes, we slam them shut. Understand what doorways are for and what they mean.

Christ even knew the importance of doorways as he said, "Knock, and it shall be open." What are your doors, and what will those doors open or close.

Behold, I stand at the door and knock.
If anyone hears my voice and opens the door, I will come to him and eat with him and he with me. I have set an open door before you, which no one can shut.

9 - YOU GET WHAT YOU PAY FOR

As mentioned, I've been the Chamber of Commerce president for many years. When potential new members talk to me about membership, I give them the details and discuss benefits. I have this policy that they choose whatever membership they want. It's not based on the number of employees, the size of the company, or other factors. I developed this policy and other concepts like how a member would want it structured rather than traditional methods usually operated by chambers.

In my past roles, I had sat on numerous boards. I belonged to nearly 20 chambers, sitting on four-chamber boards simultaneously. As a member, I didn't agree with some of the methods that seemed to be more about building the chamber's empire than the members. In fact, to the best of my knowledge, we are the only chamber that suspended membership payments during COVID for over a year to help our members during that period.

Well, during the dialogue at the end, I usually close by telling them they can pick any level they want depending upon what benefits they want or need. It doesn't matter to me. However, I remind them, "You get what you pay for". I further elaborate that the bottom tier may be fine for them to attend events, meet other members, and basic benefits. More elaborate requests, such as travel for business development, aren't covered at that level. I also further explain, and please don't think you're the first potential member to try and buy the lowest level and then whine or manipulate, thinking you will stretch it into the rest. My simple comparison is don't buy a coach ticket that generally has you sitting at the back of the plane, only served peanuts and water. Then, look in first class and see they get all the personal attention and serve champagne. They paid for it, and that's what they wanted. You are still riding in the plane, part of the flight, and getting where you need to go. I also reassure them they can always upgrade at any time with their membership applied to the higher membership. I think it's fair.

I have several stories about how some of those situations have played out, but that could be an entire book. My second book will probably mention a few of the unique projects I encountered. But for now, my point is sometimes you get what you pay for and pick, so don't complain when you can't manipulate or abuse the situation to get more. That advice includes business, life and relationship interactions in life.

Let me begin with a promotion I received from an airline. And yes, another airline story, but you must admit they give you a lot of great examples in business. My airline experiences haven't been all bad. I have some excellent airline stories and have had great experiences with one of my chamber's most extended members, United Airlines.

Due to my extensive travel, I belong to frequent flyer programs. Because of one, I recently got an "offer" sent to me for my birthday month. Ok, that's a good marketing plan because people frequently do some traveling or unique things for their birthday, so at first, I thought – well played. So, I started reading the offer. If I booked a flight during this period, they defined that after the flight, they would give me a $25 credit toward my next flight. I stopped right there. Let me get this right. I don't just get a $25 credit for my birthday immediately to use. I must book a flight and then another flight before I get anything. Lucky me. I didn't get that birthday present. How would you feel if someone gave you a gift card for your birthday as a present and it was for you to spend your money at their store? Then, the next time you came in to spend more money, once again at their store, you would get your "present." That would probably amount to less than 10% of what you spent and collectively 1-5% of the total after the two visits. No thanks.

Let's view this from the two sides of the WIN-WON concept. As an individual, consumer, or client, you must make decisions AFTER you understand what you're getting or need from the transaction or situation. This principle applies to everything from buying a car to an online membership and even a relationship. Are you trying to unfairly manipulate the situation or person(s) without intending to provide what you expected? Although you may have developed this attitude, you are good at manipulating and getting what you want. If you are unaware, I assure you other people will see and know that about you. And if not already, you will not be included in opportunities or offers at some point because they know you are one-sided and selfish.

They can only expect you to manipulate or abuse a situation or relationship in your best interest and will and probably are, leaving a wake of the carnage of disgruntled employees, customers, friends, family, and partners.

The title of this chapter is a cliché, and it relates to another saying – *if it looks too good to be true, it probably is.*

If it wasn't worth paying a good price, you should have never bought it!

10 - WAIT FOR IT...

As a Vice President of Marketing, I had a marketing budget that allowed me to purchase season tickets to the Houston Rockets, the Astros, the Houston Rodeo, and many other sporting and area events. I would use them for promotional giveaways, incentives, and various marketing strategies.

There were great perks and opportunities; however, many people eventually knew I had access to tickets to almost everything in the Houston area. I would get calls and requests continuously for tickets. People who couldn't even spell my name correctly would act like we went way back, and they would ask me for tickets for them and even people I didn't know.

The generous budget also allowed me to sponsor various events and causes. Quickly, the calls and emails came in asking me for donations. Yes, that was an essential part of the job – community relations. Still, almost every interaction eventually involved a request asking for something. In my mind, I would think, wait for it…wait for it. And yes, finally, the proposal would come. Most of the time, after a brief empty series of compliments or storylines.

After this title, I was a chamber president, assisting members, organizations, and companies with various requests. In no time, it too resulted in my thoughts – wait for it…wait for it.

The requests eventually blended into my everyday life. Even when I was a guest for dinner or in foreign countries, I knew there was an agenda, and the compliments and pampering all came with strings or a catch. What bothered me most was that people seemed to act like I wasn't on to them, or they were very clever. I was surprised to find out how smoothly they were maneuvering to get to my contacts or use me somehow.

Even in my relationships, after I disclose this or how I usually can discern what's coming, they too would work angles. Again, the insult that I didn't know what they were doing bothered me most.

A few of those people used to abuse my generosity or giving nature, even knowing I was standing there and thinking the mantra as they began their buildup to pop the question.

I enjoy helping people, especially in fulfilling their dreams and objectives.

It is something my personality needs and craves and is evident from the bookcases and walls full of awards for precisely doing that. It's the desire to help or be liked or accepted. A panel of psychologists can develop all kinds of classifications and definitions to describe it.

Interacting with people and members, sometimes, I would cut them off jokingly and tell them it was ok to ask. That was my job, so a drawn-out strategy was optional to get to the request.

Travel and business abroad to countries such as Mexico and China were the most outstanding examples of elaborate protocols and meetings before getting to the point of business.

I remember a trip to China once. My Chinese hosts gave me great favor and elite treatment at meetings, Tiananmen Square, The Forbidden City, elaborate dinners, and ground interaction at the Terracotta Army. Other rare indulgences included my private tour of a militarized zone of the Great Wall and tours of personal

and national treasures and collections not even seen by the citizens of China.

One of the most memorable was the first Westerner allowed to don the former Emperor of China's pearl necklace, which he wore only at Court to receive special guests—a necklace made by hand with 110 perfect 10mm pearls.

I remember it as one of my life's most cautious and nervous moments. I am grateful for these rare occasions and still in awe of the many "wait for it" moments.

Ask yourself if you are working the angles to maneuver to take advantage, manipulate, or gain favor for your agenda and objectives. You may be the one who always gets stuck with the check or hesitates at times to answer the phone, wondering what request is on the other end of the line.

Being the person always requesting with no intention of repayment or reciprocating the favors, services, or value may seem like sport or have you believing you are way cleverer than those around you or in business. I assure you that others have your number and know your intentions. At what cost of friendships and integrity are you leaving in your wake to those you come across? Your behavior and personality manifest in your personal and family relationships. Being this way doesn't bother you, and you don't mind that when you leave a room, it's like everyone stops holding their breath. Can you look in the mirror or even avert your stare because it feels like you need to shower to wash off the grime of guilt and selfish indulgence?

Stop and make a list for yourself that no one must see, but be honest and authentic about those to whom you owe a lot of repayment, whether it be of material value or just personal consideration and gratitude. Let people see a change in you, forging a new standard of ethics and conduct.

And draw a line in the sand for those who see the queue of people awaiting their turn at your well, which is endless and numbing. Stop the hemorrhaging of your assets, your value, and your energy. If those people stop coming around you, they aren't genuine and coming for you anyway. Let them go and recapture your integrity, self-worth, and peace of mind. Some people are good at being on the receiving end of friendships and relationships.

The interchange between you and them will never come. It may be difficult, and they may even project their problem of one-sided behavior as somehow your character flaw but cut the rope. No matter what you are providing or giving away, it comes at a price to you or something. And as I write in the chapter about time, there is an endless line of those who will gladly spend your time for you. Some will only stop draining you of assets, ideas, or favors once you stop the flow.

This part of the dialogue or interaction is where I usually hear, "Well, it's not that easy" or "It's complicated." Have you made it that way, or have they made it to ensure you feel locked into the trap? It's time to make it easy and uncomplicate things. If you are the one always providing the resources or the safety net, then you are the one with the power to stop it or control it. You may have helped them temporarily, but at a certain point, you are just enabling them, and you are not the solution but the cause.

Please list the people or situations draining you and *what* they are draining from you.

Next, draw the lines I mentioned and list when you intend it to stop and the possible outcome. Once the reality of the process is in writing and you've detailed it, the task won't seem so abstract or "complicated," and you can begin. If you don't, your mind and spirit will always be in reserve or on defense as you constantly hear the words in your head...wait for it, wait for it.

Protect yourself from people who only show up with buckets to draw from your well and never provide the rain to refill it.

11 - DECISIONS

Changing doesn't take a traumatic experience, a New Year's resolution, or moving to a new location. It just acts—a decision to do something different or try another way. And if you don't make the decision – well, you still did because you decided not to act or change anything, so you might as well try the decision for something new or different.

It's the same principle if you don't ask for a sale, date, or raise. If you don't do anything or try, you already have the "NO," but if you do ask or test, you might get a "YES." It sounds almost comically logical, but it's true.

Decisions, even minor ones, can have a significant impact on our lives and may even change the trajectory of our future. I used an illustration for my sons when they were little to show how a slight change of focus or even a little decision can get you off course and change your direction, where you end up, or your goals. I would apply that to their decisions about choosing friends, doing the wrong thing, or taking the wrong path. I would take two pieces of yarn, put them side by side, and stretch them out about 20 feet. At first, they were perfectly parallel and had the same start and stopping points. I would then take one, move it just a half inch at the base, and lay string along its new trajectory. At the start, the two lines/lives/choices were very close, and it seemed like very little change, but as the strings progressed 20 feet, by the end of the series, the two pieces of the yarn were now feet apart.

I would show my sons that even a little decision can take your life in a new direction, and now you will no longer end up where you were headed. But the best part was I would take the current string off course, show it was flexible, and show my sons how it could be redirected back onto the right path when it was getting feet apart from the other line.

I would also use that illustration regarding our beliefs about God forgiving us and allowing us to change and return on the right course. It may seem simple, but that visual demonstration illustrated the lesson to little boys.

Our lives and decisions are like that. Sometimes, however, you do want to decide to change course. Like the string, sometimes all it takes is one little decision to start, and more and more, you will take steps to make a significant directional change in your life.

Keep focused on your goals, which I cover in more detail in the chapter, Stick to the Plan. The main objective of this chapter is to help you sometimes realize that the decisions we make are necessary and may impact those we care about around us. Still, ultimately, it is just you, in the end, who determines if the decisions you make are good, inadequate, selfish, reckless, or successful. Decisions you make may impact your life or even if you live, and depending upon your beliefs, they could impact eternity.

I have had a couple of close calls, and one came during the world dilemma of COVID-19. Now, I will be the first to admit I have had a very cavalier life about how I approach things, and I like that about myself.

I live life fully and am bold about my decisions. Well, when COVID hit, and the description of its symptoms came out, it sounded like something I had already experienced in February before the world shut down. I had been on a multi-country trip in Europe and thought I caught it while abroad, and my body had already recovered from it. Now, realize this was within the first few months of COVID before we knew much about it or realized the devastating effect it was about to have on the globe.

As healthcare supplies became needed and scarce and people were afraid to go near others, I actively started helping countries and people secure products, donating masks, and supplies. I even picked up a good friend who, having been treated for COVID at a hospital, was ready to be released; no one, including taxis, would come to pick him up to return home. He called me, and without hesitation, as I had no doubt this close friend would have done it for me, I jumped in my car and went to the hospital to get him home.

At some point, COVID-19 caught back up with me and showed no mercy. Within a few days, I had to sleep upright and had difficulty breathing. I witnessed my oxygen levels slumping into the 70-80% range. Finally, one night around 3 am, my son saw me struggling and made me go to the emergency room. He had to leave me and could not stay due to COVID protocols activated in hospitals. I was taken back to the ER and given tests and a chest X-ray of my lungs. All the staff wore medical versions of hazmat suits at a distance unless necessary. At about 5 am, I received a call on my cell phone from the front desk, which I thought was very odd. They couldn't come back and ask me the questions. Then, to put things into perspective, they asked if I had a will created.

I informed them I did, and they asked if my son could bring a copy to the hospital to have on file. That shook me with the realization of mortality.

I waited several minutes, and finally, the doctor showed up but stayed at the room entrance. He would not approach me or come near me. He said your X-rays and tests came back. I said I had a good idea of the results before he started, considering he was standing at the door. And the front desk had just called asking for a will to be placed on file.

He ventured on that my lungs were saturated with COVID, as he put it, and it resembled that of double pneumonia. I was going to be taken to the COVID floor in the hospital and "kept comfortable." Wow, that's an odd way to say it other than keeping comfortable until I die. I wasn't quite sure how to take the doctor's vague medical terms.

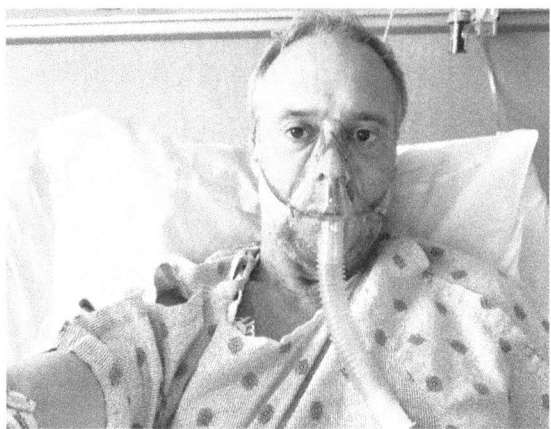
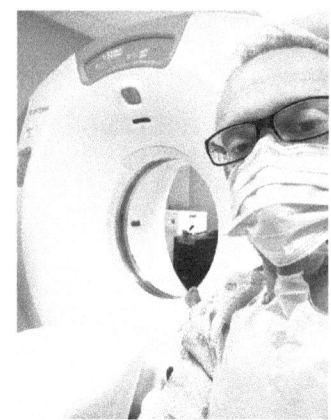

Rolling upstairs was like Moses parting the Red Sea; when people saw me coming, they parted and took extreme measures not to be remotely close to me. The feeling I know all COVID patients felt as it began isolating the world.

Medical staff took me to the farthest room from everyone at the end of a hallway. Its ventilation system was configured to operate from the window of my room. I was started on oxygen and given some antibiotics. Remember, it was just a few months after the global shutdown, and the medical community was still scrambling on just how to treat this illness.

Every medical person who came in wore a hazmat suit and placed everything I touched or used in a toxic waste medical bag for disposal. There was this kind of nature to everyone, but it was also as though they were treating an alien and were in awe of what might happen next.

The medical staff checked oxygen every 20-30 minutes, and the discussion began about whether I needed intubation as I was on the maximum amount of oxygen. I continued politely arguing that I wanted to stay awake and fight as long as I could before they did that. It would be lights out, and then maybe I would awake better or not at all. I had decided to stay awake and fight for my life.

Fighting to stay awake after being up for a few days without sleep, in fear of falling asleep and not waking up or them intubating me, I realized I should come to terms with this and start making calls. I still had my cell phone, so I began calling family to reassure them and downplay what was happening. Unknown to them, I was saying goodbye. I called my three sons, saving my youngest, til the very last because I wanted to take off my oxygen mask so he could see my face and not be as worried or not have his last memory of me in the mask, grasping to breathe. I remember trying to load up on oxygen and breathing deep several times like I was getting ready to hold my breath underwater. I called him and took the mask off before he could see it. The call was brief, but I was cavalier and hoped to reassure him.

I told him I had to go because the nurses were coming in. Which they were because without the oxygen on, my oxygen percentage was quickly dropping on their monitoring machines, and they thought I was quickly diving.

Reluctantly, I said goodbye and then felt the tears building after I knew he was off the phone and could no longer see my face. I explained to the two medical staff what I had done and was doing, and they politely scolded me but got me stable and left the room.

Then, several things came rushing to mind. That was the last call or face of a loved one I would ever see. I began to feel sorry for older people who I realized must be isolated like me. Those patients, however, may not have phones to tell everyone goodbye. And the isolation and feeling of death that may be creeping over them and the fear they must be coping with besides the health struggle itself. I felt very calm and thankful that because of traveling abroad so much alone, I don't fear being alone and like being alone quite often. I wondered if all of that had been to prepare me for this very moment in retrospect.

I then started to recall and search for my past and life. I began wondering if there was anything I would have done differently or, in fact, anyone else I needed to call and apologize to or tell them I loved them because I missed the opportunity. I thought about all the classic movies where people get a re-do because they didn't do things right or would have made different decisions.

It was odd, but I searched and considered several things, like past relationships, friends, etc. And then I got an amazing calm and peace over me. I realized the only thing I would change is spending more time with my sons.

I realized, however, that at some point, I would leave their life due to death, and so that would always be a wish, but just how life transpires. I then thought about all the things I had gotten to do, called to see, brought to experience. A warm flood of tears started again because instead of fear or anger for my situation, I felt so humbled and grateful to God for the life I had. I did it right. I could tell myself I did it right. That was the most liberating moment in my life. I realized some people never get to experience that feeling or know until the last minute of life, and then it's too late. They might then slip off into eternity with the sense of what if or if I should have done things differently. I wasn't going to have that.

I was content, and again, even knowing I had made many mistakes, I had revered them, forgiven anyone I felt had wronged me, and most importantly, I had lived life and raged, as I call it, for every adventure and second, I could get out of it.

As I begin closing this book, I hope you will make changes if necessary, and you can assess if you have lived your fullest life or if it is time to start. More than anything, that's what I want you to take away from this.

I turned the corner the next day, and within a few days, I left the hospital. I have no doubt it was from the faith I and those around me caring for me at the hospital. My body quickly recovered with nothing more than vitamins, antibiotics, and steroids. The healthcare industry had no drugs that were trusted and tried yet.

And for those of you with faith, I want to leave you with one last story to close. On a trip to the Holy Land around 2012, I was in Jerusalem and coming to the tour close.

I had seen Nazareth, Bethlehem, the Sea of Galilee, the Dead Sea, the Temple, the Wailing Wall, and the Garden of Gethsemane. I even got re-baptized in the Jordan River. We had just come from an area believed to be Golgotha and were sitting in an area proposed as one of the sites that may have been Christ's burial tomb.

I had read the bible since I was 13, so I was familiar with all the stories. However, when you grow up like that, I must admit that sometimes it becomes understood, accepted, and not necessarily agreed with or believed. Having spent over a week walking in the same places Christ and disciples had and hearing the stories again, seeing the surroundings to make them come to life was very surreal. I've heard about their diverse characters and non-impressive attitudes. When we are sitting and listening to the story of the resurrection, and although I have heard this story many times, especially at Easter every year, something finally hits me.

These average or even questionable men who came from an assortment of pasts and cowards when Christ needed them most had not only denied him but had gone into hiding. They were scared, bewildered, and probably just waiting for things to quiet down to sneak out of town and wander into oblivion.

But something that made them change and become fearless and confident of what they had seen and experienced had to happen. For the remainder of their lives, they were focused and unafraid.

Just being honest about human nature – I decided something had to happen to them.

When you put this book down, although I hope you will return to it occasionally, I hope you and those important to you stay focused and become fearless. Based upon whatever you naturally lean toward or call upon. I can only give you mine as a benchmark, but you must decide and find yours.

Ensure that whenever your checkbook of time has run out, say Whew, that was a ride; that was all I could get in, and every bit of it was well spent.

Time is your only commodity in life. Spend it Wisely; let no one take it from you freely; value others' time and spend or share your time with those who value you and your time.

12 - STICK TO THE PLAN

Writing a book has been a dream of mine for years.

And I've used my experiences as the basis for reference. I hope it has not come across as a self-absorbed journal. If you are one of the people reading this who knows me well, you know that's not how I am.

I am blessed and have gotten to travel and see and do some fantastic things in my life. And for that, I am very grateful. I show the pictures when I'm traveling for multiple reasons. Believe it or not, the least of these is to say, "Oh, look at me." I hope they entice or motivate people to travel, try new things, and get out and live. Wear a red dress; dance in the rain or whenever the music is playing; smell the roses; play with your kids; don't take anything for granted.

Writing this is a little scary, as telling stories about yourself or experiences opens a person up to judgment or naysayers who may not wish the best for you or, by any means, be happy with your achievements.

I have had my share, and I have experienced betrayal many times. I have a phrase I've coined over the years – *I have so many knives in my back that I ran out of room, so I had to turn around, but at least I can see it coming now.* Ever feel that way?

I grew up in a big family. We are all very close. I have four brothers and a sister, with me being the youngest. My brothers are my best friends. My sister was the oldest and 12 years apart from me. She was a combination of my sister, like a mom, and my best friend. She was the closest person in the world to me. I lost her to cancer in March of 2023 after she gallantly fought for over a decade.

My parents divorced when I was eight, so I never spent much time with either one. But with four older brothers, that whole male bonding, learning sports, and having stability was well covered.

Our household had only a little money, but we had everything we needed. I always liked being active and working, and I had my first job when I was seven.

I had a paper route. I was technically too young to have it, but one of my older brothers had it, and when he was ready to stop, I just took it over.

From that time on, I have been writing down my goals. I would cut out pictures of things I wanted or hoped to have and achieve at different periods. All I knew was I had to stick to the plan.

I was very active in school, especially in high school. Active in sports and even became student body president. My experience there was exceptional. I grew up with great friends and still talk to them today, as well as teachers who significantly impacted my life. I even text or speak to some of them regularly. I came across the classic book by Napoleon Hill, Think and Grow Rich, and read it at 16. It had a significant impact and influence on my life, and even now, I hope that if this book is read by just one person that it influences as he did me, I will consider it a success. I don't need to sell millions of copies; I hope it impacts a few people, and I'm good.

The ride you take in life is yours, and many people, willingly or unintentionally, will impact or could change your life.

So, for the good and some unfortunately for the bad. Remember, it's YOUR life, and regardless of what you go through, only one person will be there through it all with you – YOURSELF. I somehow understood that concept early. And I'm glad I did. I grew to like being around me.

I tell people, "I like me." Another expression I use is, "Some days it's good to be me"."

It's essential that you like YOU. You can look at yourself in the mirror every day and still not be looking at yourself. You need to like yourself even when you fail, when you hurt someone you care about, or when someone you care about hurts you.

You don't need to be selfish about it, narcissistic, or egomaniacal. Still, it would help to be proud of yourself and what you accomplished, whether great or small. Give yourself permission to fail and realize your past is not a prison; it's just practice. Don't condemn yourself, and don't condemn those around you. Give other people as much grace and forgiveness as you want. That's fair – right?

Give yourself permission and encouragement to try new things and adventure. Don't let others keep you in a box, and especially don't do it to yourself. Why are you busy thinking people are watching or judging you? I hate to tell you, but they are so wrapped up in their multiverse that they probably aren't even noticing you. And if they are, don't worry; tomorrow, there will be another news cycle, and they will focus on something else. Don't let that statement get you down as to say I'm just not significant enough for someone to care about or notice. Realize that it allows you to be adventurous and go after your dreams. Remember the chapter on viewpoints. You need to have the correct view of yourself and look at the advantages, not the limitations.

I saw a great example on Facebook recently, where a violinist named Joshua Bell played in a New York subway for 45 minutes and only earned about $30 in tips while playing some of the most impressive pieces. He was playing these pieces with a violin valued at 3.5 million dollars. Yet a few days earlier, he had played in a sold-out Boston theater for a show with tickets starting at $100.

Another great example is if you buy a bottle of water at the grocery store, it's about $1. If you purchase it in a convenience store, it's about $2. When you buy it at the airport, it's $5—same brand, the same bottle of water, just different locations and different perceived values. You need to understand that your brand is good and valuable; you may just be selling it in the wrong place.

You also need to understand that life isn't a sprint; it's a marathon, and you must make every part of the race enjoyable and memorable. Sometimes, your success is a progression; sometimes, a position, job, or experience may not be where you want to end up, but it may be what you need to help get you there.

I tell my sons to try some things because failure at trying is still one step closer to finding what they do like or want to end up with. Write down your goals and journal, or mark and note the progress.

Even if that progress is what you perceive to be going backward. *It's easier to hit a target if you know what you're aiming at.* In the meantime, enjoy the ride because it's life happening right before your eyes.

In my second book, already underway, I will focus on some of my adventures and the people I got to run into and hang out with just along my ride because I wasn't waiting for life to come to me. I was out going after it. Some included Brad Pitt, Reese Witherspoon, Daniel Craig, ZZ Top, Billy Idol, Red Hot Chili Peppers, and Willie Nelson, not to mention numerous professional athletes, billionaires, world leaders, and royalties. And it wasn't just brushing up against them in a line or on the street. There were moments and hours of hanging out with them, getting to talk to them like the people they are, and they were all just along my road of adventures and almost all very unexpected. I know, though, that they wouldn't show up at my house if I had just waited for them.

I get asked often about how I got where I am and what I did to get here. I enjoy telling people, hoping to motivate them to see, do, and try more. Now, I admit, if you want to find faults in me or things I may have done wrong. I have my share. Geroge Clooney once said if he ran for a political office, he would have to run on the "Yep, I did It" platform. I hate to steal his line, but I'm right there with him. I'm not perfect and have made mistakes, but I never stopped.

Many opportunities and rare moments happened in my journey as I got to my goals and showed me how sometimes one thing will lead to another.

It was a natural progression that flowed, but my sons call it my nine lives like I'm some cat.

At an early age, I used to dance with my sister, who loved dancing, and it stayed with me. I somehow got into some of the classes at the local college to participate because my mom knew the instructor. When I was 12, a dance company from New York came to perform—and heard about me from the college instructor, who had me come and dance for them.

I didn't know what was going on, so I did. The next day, I heard a conversation between my mom and the instructor that the company wanted me to move to New York because I had talent. Let's face it: there weren't too many boys who could dance by 12 at that time.

Considering the strict religion, I grew up in, that wasn't about to happen. Fine by me, a professional dancer wasn't the most popular choice as a boy; I was getting into baseball. But it would show up again later. My former classmates and friends throughout my life, if you asked them, seem always to be one thing they remember about me – my dancing.

I enjoyed art in high school because one of my brothers was good, and I just wanted to draw with him as a kid. I had two outstanding art teachers who were great mentors and teachers. I won national art awards and started selling my art by age 15, which evolved into an interest in art, design, and fashion that later developed into many other things.

Then, when I combined dancing and art, I developed an interest in modeling. At 16, I got training, especially with an interest in runway modeling, because of the dancing. I signed up with John Casablanca's in Kansas City. I did local ads like the Jones Store, Bass Pro, some TV, and teen runway shows. Missouri projects that were local and regional. That is good enough for me. Unfortunately, my staggering height of only 5'8" meant I wouldn't do high fashion runway. Feeling like I was all artsy for my age, I started writing poetry and getting published by 18.

I enjoyed acting in high school and did theater productions in college, where the instructor would let me choreograph my routines in musicals – again with the dancing. Also, during college, I engaged in my curiosity for martial arts. I earned advanced belts in karate, Tae kwon do, and judo.

Then, out of college, I moved to Nashville, Tennessee, to be near my sister and take on roles I enjoyed.

I signed up with a modeling agency there because, by this time, I had accumulated a lot of experience and become an instructor for the men's and some kids' programs. Interestingly enough, that's where I taught Reese Witherspoon when she was about 12 or 13.

I met and hung out with numerous singers and celebrities during that period. I also picked up a merchandising role with Ralph Lauren, the icon for the 80's. I was living the life. And if that wasn't enough, I had a chance to join a dance company where I got trained and picked up more traditional dance and even learned ballroom dances like the waltz, tango, rumba, cha cha, foxtrot, samba, paso doble, and others into silver and gold levels of dance. Eventually, it allowed me to dance with MTV at an event in Nashville called City Lights.

I'll skip ahead, and eventually, I ended up in Houston, Texas. I applied everything I had learned to date, kept advancing my martial arts training to get my black belt in Tae Kwon Do, and added advanced belts in Aikido. With those, I eventually taught six martial arts classes in a program to help keep inner-city youth out of gangs.

During this period, I was able to operate my own company that did special events and merchandising. I built a client list, including shopping centers, and coordinated several fashion shows monthly. Including work with *Teen Magazine* and one of my favorite shows with Daisy Fuentes, a trendy pop culture icon at the time. In total, I coordinated over 200 fashion shows in my modeling career. Also, having taught over an estimated 2,000 models before I stepped away from the modeling industry, I could argue during that period, I was one of the top male runway instructors in the nation. The agency in Houston, where I taught the men's division in the mid-90s, had my protégés winning male runway pro and semi-pro for three years straight at the Modeling Association of America International (MAAI) in New York.

In the meantime, my skills from my merchandising company were getting noticed, and I got recruited to assist with new store designs.

Reggie Gray

REGGIE GRAY

This opportunity allowed me to apply the art skills I had developed in high school, my fashion background from modeling and Ralph Lauren, my love of the outdoors, and extensive travel. The opportunity would find me getting "paid to play," as I called it, and contribute to what would eventually lead to three different design award teams for three other companies: Oshman's, The North Face, and Bass Pro.

At Oshman's, I began applying my experience in art and photography from being in modeling, and my outdoor and action photos ended up in stores all over the US. My time at The North Face was equally exciting, as I got to hang out and learn rock climbing from world-renowned climbers like Pete Athans, Conrad Anker, and Alex Lowe. Then, to close out my outdoor career, I got to work with billionaire Johnny Morris, founder of Bass Pro and Missouri icon, where I had grown up. We laughed a few times about how I had gone from modeling his pool toys when I was younger to flying around the country, researching, and helping to plan his new stores all over the US.

At one point, though, I decided I was spending too much time away from home and transitioned into a position with a former client, General Growth Properties, a shopping center owner. I was soon recruited from them by a company owned by Academy Award-winning film producer Bob Yari.

As his Vice President of Marketing, I sat on numerous boards, as detailed in my author bio. After years of

marketing, I was recruited as the President of a board I had once sat on and revitalized it. That chamber was developed into an international chamber. I further developed my training in economic, community, and international development. For a brief period, I served in dual executive roles as the chamber president and the vice president of business development for a global logistics company. These roles are where my international travel has broadened over the years.

In my position, my reputation grew, and other countries' governments sought me out to assist with their economic challenges. It required meeting and interfacing with various world leaders, industries, companies, and business people.

The stories in my second book, *I May Never Come This Way Again*, comprised of these interactions, exposed me to several unique situations that evolved into my work with other government agencies, where I developed some of my now closest friends. I know several people around me are anxious for me to finally disclose some of the James Bond stories, as they call them. Stories of meeting members of the Muslim Brotherhood behind the pyramids of Cario, Egypt; meeting with an arms dealer in Malta; diamond buyers

and sellers in Zurich and Moscow. Individuals in the Grand Bazaar and Marrakesh, Morrocco. Working to release someone from a prison in the Dominican Republic or negotiating with a white-collar criminal in his cell in a Mexican Federal prison regarding $170 Million of missing funds. Or organizing meetings with the new President and his administration of Panama and a US agency regarding preventative measures against corruption before the Summit of the Americas. The humor to me looking back at pictures posted is that to most, when viewed, thought, "Oh how nice Reggie is traveling again," not realizing they were disclosing locations or leaving breadcrumbs of my possible location for others viewing, in the event a project didn't go well.

One of the great opportunities created was an invitation to participate in the Federal Bureau of Investigation's community program, the Citizens Academy. In the FBICA organization, I held the position of President for an unprecedented four years. I chaired many projects for them, receiving several awards and acknowledgments from Directors Mueller and Comey and meeting FBI icons such as Joe Pistone and Frank Abagnale. Johnny Depp played Agent Joe Pistone in *Donnie Brasco*, and

Leonardo DiCaprio played Frank Abagnale in *Catch Me If You Can*.

As you see, where you start and end up can be an incredible ride. Your life happens the entire time, and you collect experience, contacts, and abilities. Gather all you can and focus on what you want and where you want to be, not only in that stage of your life but in the future.

By writing this book, I disclosed many personal life events, opening my privacy to many I may not know. The history given is not to boast but to remind the reader that I'm an average guy with average height and looks who took risks, seized opportunities, and lived my excitement and dreams. There is no celebrity appeal status here or abundance of wealth. Still, it was just a satisfying history of no regrets, and no opportunity passed. My challenge is that if I can do so many things that are fulfilling to me, and in my definition of success and happiness, there is no reason you cannot pursue the same. The only person who is setting limitations on you IS YOU.

Your past is not a prison; it's a practice.

ABOUT THE AUTHOR

Reggie Gray is a seasoned professional with a robust career spanning more than two decades in economic development, marketing, and international business. As the President of the Intercontinental Chamber of Commerce for 18 years, Gray has been a pivotal figure in the Houston area, with a strong presence in the community for over 25 years. His extensive experience includes serving on numerous boards, contributing to community development, and earning a multitude of awards for his dedication and service to the Houston-area communities.

Prior to his tenure at the Chamber, Reggie held significant roles in the real estate management and development industry as a Vice President of

Marketing and in the international logistics sector as a Vice President of Business Development. His diverse projects and positions have seen him travel throughout the United States and to nearly 60 countries globally, where he has worked alongside a range of industries, corporate executives, international leaders, and royalty.

Gray's commitment to economic and community development is reflected in his involvement with prestigious organizations such as the International Economic Development Council (IEDC), the International Council of Shopping Centers (ICSC), and the Community Development Institute. His leadership roles include serving as President of the FBI Citizens Academy Alumni Association and as a delegate to FBI National Conferences.

Gray is a member of multiple advisory councils and boards of directors, including the Small Business Development Center Advisory Council and various chambers of commerce. His contributions to public service and economic growth have been recognized with numerous awards, including a City of Houston Proclamation declaring "Reggie Gray Day," FBI service awards, and several community service accolades.

In addition to his professional endeavors, Reggie Gray has collaborated on projects as a Texas Licensed Private Investigator, showcasing a diverse skill set that complements his expansive career. His dedication to the community is further exemplified by his voluntary leadership in charitable organizations like the Juvenile Diabetes Research Foundation and Feed the Children, among others. Reggie Gray's career is characterized by a passion for development, a commitment to service, and an impressive track record of fostering international partnerships and community growth.

Gray's diverse roles have enabled him to meet global leaders and personalities while traveling the world. This has also allowed him to collaborate and be a resource for government agencies, which has led to numerous experiences and adventures that he applies to speaking and business opportunities. Gray is currently working on another book describing some of these unique experiences. However, Gray still spends time and speaks often of his three sons and his focus on them or, as he has repeatedly been quoted, "They are the oxygen in his lungs."

For more information and to connect with Reggie Gray visit: HoustonICC.org/book

www.ingramcontent.com/pod-product-compliance
Lightning Source LLC
Chambersburg PA
CBHW051530120626
46551CB00012B/1164